# BLESSED & HIGHLY FLAVORED

To Michelle,

Enjoy the book!

Diaz

# A LEGACY OF SOUTHERN FAMILY COOKING

## DIAZ ALLEN

# BLESSED & HIGHLY FLAVORED

## Rags N Riches™
### PUBLISHING

Published in 2013 by Rags N Riches Publishing, a Division of Rags N Riches Enterprises.

ISBN-13: 978-1-4820-5201-5

Printed in the United States

Text by Diaz Allen & Raphael Baker
Design by Diaz Allen
Edited by Raphael Baker
Cover & Contents Page Photography by J.R. West
Food Images & Styling by Diaz Allen

www.diazallen.com

# To My 'Bran-Ma'

Thank you for assisting my mother in my up-bringing. You told me it was okay to be an individual and be different. Thank you for teaching me responsibility, how to love, and how to be loved. Thank you for paving the way that allowed me to follow my dreams. I love you! (I would say "See you soon"... but I can wait.)

*My grandmother and I in the kitchen at Aunt Grace and Uncle Eddie's (former) home in Maryland! (1982)*

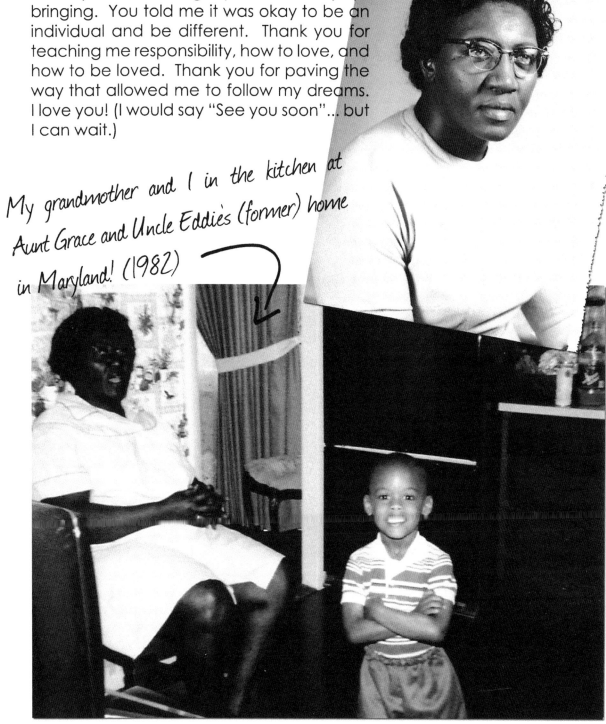

Grandma, Grandpa, and my mother!

My mother at work while she was pregnant with me in 1978.

An article about my grandfather Walter's music writing!

Me!

**GOINGS ON**
BY Raymond Lowery

A WHOLE lot of song-writing's going on in the Raleigh area these days—for better or worse—and the newest team of composer and lyricist is Walter B. Allen and Irving Fuller, both of the Chavis Heights section.

Allen, 34, Middleburg native who is a graduate of the State School for the Blind here, has turned out the words for four pop tunes, namely: "Cheer Up, Pretty One," "Buzz Me on the Telephone," "Didn't I Tell You So," and "Newcomer."

His lyrics were set to music by Fuller, 24-year-old Raleigh native, who is a sophomore and music major at North Carolina College in Durham.

Now a couple of the songs—"Cheer Up, Pretty One," with "Buzz Me On the Telephone" on the flip side—have been recorded by Renown Records of New York City at its Durham office and have reached the music stores in this area. The other tunes have also been recorded, but they haven't been released yet.

All of the Allen-Fuller efforts were recorded by the Corvettes, a popular instrumental combo, and feature Fuller on the vocals as well as on tenor and alto sax.

Fuller, who has been composing music for several years, has been the leader of 10 bands since he started to high school. He is unmarried.

Allen, who is blind, is the author of a book of poems, "Moods on Parade," which was published in 1954. He is married and the father of a three-year-old daughter.

The Allen-Fuller record is being "plugged" by several disc jockeys in and around Raleigh.

NOV • 63

My Cousin Manda, my Great-Grandmother Vera, and my Mother!

# CONTENTS

# FOREWORD by CAROLYN ALLEN

As a young mother, I found it important to ensure that my son, Diaz, and his grandparents had a close relationship. I think that my parents' generation was a group of people that still understood the importance of going the extra mile.

My father, Walter, was totally blind for most of his life. He never let his hurdle become a barrier. He became one of the first people of color to own a store in downtown Raleigh, NC. My mother, Juanita, had a number of health issues. She suffered from vision and respiratory problems. Yet, she never played victim. She worked until she physically was no longer able.

Both of my parents took on the responsibility of teaching my son the basics of being an adult. They taught him about education, working to make a living, paying bills, and maintaining a household.

All of their lessons still show in his life today. Diaz is educated, hard working, responsible, and can cook a mouth-watering meal. There are a couple of dishes that I have stopped cooking because I have tasted how good his version is.

I thank God every day for allowing my son to have been able to spend quality time with his grandparents. We have been a very blessed and highly favored family. The recipes that my son shares in this book are Blessed and Highly Flavored!

# BLESSED

Some of my favorite memories from childhood involve me and my Grand-mother in her kitchen. As a small child, I would watch in amazement as my Grandmother glided around the kitchen. She sang hymns and had a slight smile on her face. When she would finally sit down, there was a mouth-watering meal waiting for the family on top of her stove.

When I grew tall enough to reach the stovetop, my Grandmother sat me down for a serious conversation. Her bright blue eyes seemed to gaze through me as she said, "Son, you are going to learn to cook for yourself. These women are not teaching their girls how to boil water. If you learn to cook, then you will never have to depend on these "new women" to feed you."

From that point on, my Grandmother directed me in the kitchen like it was a stage play. Sometimes it even seemed like a boot camp. While the neighborhood children would play outside until it was time for dinner, I often had to go inside early to make dinner.

Over a period of about eight years, my Grandmother drilled the art of cooking into me. She would explain to me that cooking for your family and friends is a great way to show your love. Cooking takes time and patience. Anyone can eat out, but not everyone can provide a delicious home cooked meal.

I truly appreciate my mother for leaving me in the care of my Grandmother. I am Blessed! So many people do not have a relationship with their grand-parents. Some have never even met them. My Grandmother passed away when I was sixteen. In her lifetime, she gave me the greatest gift I have ever received. She gave me the gift of cooking.

# HIGHLY FLAVORED

Those of us who have been able to enjoy our grandmothers' cooking often try to emulate the flavor in our own cooking. Although we can never recreate that magic, we can create our own legacy. This book is a compilation of recipes for some of the dishes that my Grandmother, Mother, and I have adopted as our signature dishes.

I have learned that the most important part of any dish is the flavor. The seasonings and spices used are a reflection of our love. Even though we can sometimes change an ingredient to put a new spin on a dish, we should always use quality ingredients to maintain the integrity of the recipe. Remember, a meal must always be flavorful.

*My Great-Grandmother Vera in her kitchen in Bentonville, NC. (1963)*

*A recipe written by my Grandmother Juanita!*

# ENTICING ENTREES

# RICH & CREAMY CHICKEN ALFREDO

**4 CUPS CHICKEN, CHOPPED**

**1 16oz JAR ALFREDO SAUCE**

**1 16oz JAR GARLIC PARMESAN SAUCE**

**4 CUPS MOZZARELLA CHEESE, SHREDDED**

**1 CUP MUSHROOMS, SLICED**

**1 LB BOWTIE PASTA**

**¼ TEASPOON SALT**

**¼ TEASPOON GROUND BLACK PEPPER**

**1 TEASPOON ITALIAN SEASONING**

**1 TEASPOON PARSLEY, CHOPPED**

**2 TEASPOONS VIRGIN OLIVE OIL**

**2 TABLESPOONS UNSALTED BUTTER**

**[ SERVES 8 ]**

1. Heat oil in large pan over medium heat.

2. Add chicken to pan and sprinkle with salt and pepper.

3. Brown chicken, then add mushrooms. Sauté chicken and mushrooms.

3. In large pot, bring 4 quarts of water to boil. Add a pinch of salt, butter, and pasta. Boil uncovered for 12-15 minutes and then drain in colander.

4. Pour sauce over chicken, add cheese, Italian seasoning, and parsley. Stir and let simmer for about 10 minutes.

5. Return pasta to pot. Pour sauce mixture over pasta. Blend well.

*I began making this dish almost five years ago, and I never imagined it would become one of my signature dishes. It is something I fell in love with at a few of my favorite restaurants, and when I make it, family and friends invite themselves over. For a delicious variation of this recipe, add grilled shrimp. This dish is guaranteed to satisfy and you may want to have pillows handy for the aftermath!*

# POP POP'S **CHICKEN POT PIE**

1 LB CHICKEN BREAST, COOKED & DICED

1/3 CUP BUTTER, MELTED

3 TABLESPOONS ALL PURPOSE FLOUR

1½ CUPS CHICKEN BROTH

2/3 CUP MILK

1 15oz CAN MIXED VEGETABLES

10 PEARL ONIONS, HALVED

½ TEASPOON KOSHER SALT

½ TEASPOON GROUND BLACK PEPPER

2 ROLLS UNBAKED 9" PIE CRUSTS

[SERVES 8]

1. Blend butter, flour, broth, and milk in pan.

2. Cook sauce over medium heat, stirring constantly, until slightly thickened.

3. Preheat oven to 350°.

4. Add chicken, vegetables, salt, and pepper to sauce. Blend well.

5. Cover 9" pie pan with one pie crust. Form crust to fit inside shape of pan. Fill pan with chicken mixture and gently cover with second crust. Use back of fork to bond two crusts together.

6. Bake until crust is golden brown.

My chicken pot pie is delicious and wholesome, and will warm your soul on a cold winter day. I include huge chunks of chicken, large pieces of potatoes and pearl onions. Pearl onions are the key. Regular onions only have a faint flavor, but pearl onions give you a large pop of flavor when you bite down into them. This was one of my grandfather's favorite dishes!

# GLORIOUSLY CHEESY **LASAGNA**

1 LB GROUND MILD PORK SAUSAGE

1 LB GROUND BEEF

12 LASAGNA NOODLES

½ MEDIUM VIDALIA ONION, CHOPPED

¼ TEASPOON GARLIC POWDER

1 24oz JAR 6 CHEESE SPAGHETTI SAUCE

1 14oz CAN ROASTED DICED TOMATOES

1 6oz CAN TOMATO PASTE

2 TABLESPOONS SUGAR

¼ TEASPOON SALT

¼ TEASPOON GROUND BLACK PEPPER

1 TEASPOON ITALIAN SEASONING

1 TABLESPOON PARSLEY, CHOPPED

15oz RICOTTA CHEESE

1 EGG, BEATEN

1 LB MOZZARELLA CHEESE, SHREDDED

8oz PARMESAN CHEESE, SHREDDED

[8-12 SERVINGS]

1. Cook sausage, beef, and onion over medium heat until well browned. Stir in tomatoes, tomato paste, and spaghetti sauce. Season with garlic, sugar, Italian seasoning, salt, pepper, and parsley. Cover and simmer for about 15 minutes, stirring occasionally.

2. Bring a large pot of lightly salted water to a boil. Cook noodles in boiling water for 8 to 10 minutes. Drain and rinse with cold water.

3. In a mixing bowl, combine ricotta and egg.

4. Preheat oven to 375°.

TIP: For a healthier alternative, use ground turkey instead of ground beef and pork sausage!

**5.** Spread 1/3 of meat sauce in the bottom of a 10x15 inch baking dish. Arrange 4 noodles lengthwise over sauce. Spread with ½ of the ricotta mixture. Top with 1/3 of mozzarella. Spoon 1/3 of sauce over mozzarella, and sprinkle with 1/4 parmesan. Repeat layers, cover with remaining noodles, mozzarella and parmesan.

**6.** Spray foil with cooking spray. Cover lasagna, sprayed side down.

**7.** Bake for 25 minutes. Remove foil, and bake an additional 25 minutes.

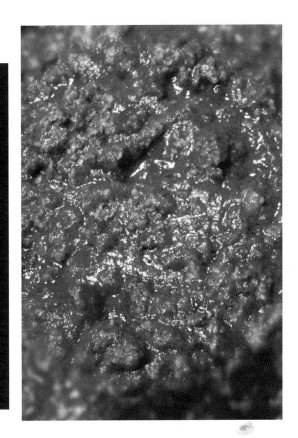

# SLOW-COOKED **POT ROAST**

1 5-6 LB BEEF ROAST

1 12oz JAR BEEF GRAVY

1 12oz JAR TURKEY GRAVY

1 PACKAGE VEGETABLE SOUP & DIP MIX

½ CUP MUSHROOMS, SLICED

½ CUP PEARL ONIONS, HALVED

½ TABLESPOON CELERY FLAKES

½ TEASPOON GROUND BLACK PEPPER

2 CUPS BEEF BROTH

1. Place beef roast in crock pot.

2. Pour the broth over and around the roast.

3. Top the roast with mix, mushrooms, onions, celery flakes, and pepper.

4. Cook on low for 7-9 hours or until tender. During last hour, pour turkey and beef gravy over and around the roast.

[8 SERVINGS]

# MOM'S **SPAGHETTI**

1 LB GROUND BEEF

1 LB GROUND MILD PORK SAUSAGE

1 CUP MUSHROOMS, SLICED

¾ BOX OF SPAGHETTI, COOKED

1 24oz JAR 6 CHEESE SPAGHETTI SAUCE

1 14oz CAN DICED ROASTED TOMATOES

1 6oz CAN TOMATO PASTE

2 TABLESPOONS GRANULATED SUGAR

1 TEASPOON SALT

¼ TEASPOON GROUND BLACK PEPPER

1 TABLESPOON PARSLEY, CHOPPED

2 CUPS CHEDDAR CHEESE, SHREDDED

[SERVES 8]

1. In large skillet, brown beef and sausage.

2. Drain, add mushrooms, sauté.

3. Add sauce, tomatoes, paste, sugar, salt, pepper, and parsley.

4. Simmer on medium heat for 20 minutes.

5. In large pot, add sauce to spaghetti and blend thoroughly.

6. Top with cheddar cheese.

# CRISPY SOUTHERN **FRIED CHICKEN**

1 CHICKEN, SECTIONED

1 CUP ALL PURPOSE FLOUR

½ TEASPOON SALT

½ TEASPOON GROUND BLACK PEPPER

1 TEASPOON CREOLE SEASONING

2 EGGS, BEATEN

1 TEASPOON HOT SAUCE

½ TEASPOON WORCESTERSHIRE SAUCE

¼ CUP CANOLA OIL

1. Combine flour, salt, pepper, and Creole seasoning in medium bowl.

2. Combine eggs, hot sauce, and Worcestershire sauce in small bowl.

3. Preheat oil in frying pan over medium heat.

4. Individually, coat each chicken piece with egg mixture, then coat with flour mixture.

5. Cook chicken in pan for 15 minutes. Turn chicken over and cook 15 more minutes.

6. Remove chicken and drain on paper towel covered plate.

[SERVES 4]

# FLAKY **FRIED FISH**

**2 LBS FISH FILLETS**

**½ TEASPOON GROUND BLACK PEPPER**

**1½ TEASPOONS CREOLE SEASONING**

**1½ CUPS SEAFOOD BREADER**

**2 CUPS CANOLA OIL**

**[SERVES 6]**

1. Cut fish into half length portions.

2. Preheat oil in frying pan over medium heat.

3. Season both sides of fish with salt, pepper, and Creole seasoning.

4. Coat fish with breader and place in frying pan.

5. Brown fish on both sides, about 5 minutes each side.

6. Remove fish and drain on paper towel covered plate.

# OVEN-BAKED **BBQ RIBS**

4 LBS SPARE RIBS (PORK OR BEEF)

1 MEDIUM VIDALIA ONION, CHOPPED

1 8oz CAN TOMATO SAUCE

½ CUP WATER

¼ CUP DARK BROWN SUGAR

¼ CUP HONEY

3 TABLESPOONS WORCESTERSHIRE SAUCE

2 TABLESPOONS YELLOW MUSTARD

2 TEASPOONS SALT

¼ TEASPOON GROUND BLACK PEPPER

¼ TEASPOON GARLIC POWDER

¼ TEASPOON CAYENNE PEPPER

¼ CUP VIRGIN OLIVE OIL

[SERVES 4-6]

1. Heat oil in large skillet on medium heat.

2. Sauté onions in skillet then add remaining ingredients.

3. Simmer on low for 15 minutes, stirring occasionally.

4. Preheat oven to 350°.

5. Place ribs in large baking pan, cover in sauce. Cover with foil.

6. Bake for 2 hours or until fork tender.

# JUICY **OVEN-FRIED CHICKEN**

---

**1 CHICKEN, SECTIONED**

**2 CUPS ALL PURPOSE FLOUR**

**½ TEASPOON GARLIC POWDER**

**1½ TABLESPOONS PARSLEY, CHOPPED**

**½ CUP BUTTER, MELTED**

**2 TEASPOONS SALT**

**½ TEASPOON GROUND BLACK PEPPER**

**1 TEASPOON HOT SAUCE**

**1 TEASPOON WORCESTERSHIRE SAUCE**

**½ CUP CANOLA OIL**

**[4 SERVINGS]**

*Everyone knows that fried chicken is a staple in the South. During the summer, my mother said it was too hot to fry chicken on top of the stove, so instead she would fry it in the oven. That way she could put it in and leave the kitchen. Oven fried chicken is much juicer and more tender than traditional fried chicken.*

1. Rinse chicken and pat dry.

2. Preheat oven to 350°.

3. Combine flour, salt, garlic, pepper, and parsley.

4. Separately combine butter, hot sauce, and Worcestershire sauce in shallow bowl.

5. Dip chicken in butter mixture and then in flour mixture.

6. Coat bottom of 9x13 inch baking dish with oil. Place chicken skin side up in dish, cover with foil, and bake for 30 minutes. Turn pieces over and bake for another 30 minutes. Remove from oven and drain on paper towels.

# SAVORY SMOTHERED **PORK CHOPS**

**4 MEDIUM PORK CHOPS**

**1 12oz JAR TURKEY GRAVY**

**½ CUP MUSHROOMS, SLICED**

**1 MEDIUM YELLOW ONION, SLICED**

**1 CUP ALL PURPOSE FLOUR**

**½ TEASPOON SALT**

**½ TEASPOON GROUND BLACK PEPPER**

**½ TEASPOON GARLIC POWDER**

**½ TEASPOON CREOLE SEASONING**

**¼ CUP CANOLA OIL**

[SERVES 4]

1. Heat oil in large pan over medium heat.

2. Season chops on both sides with Creole seasoning and garlic powder.

3. Coat chops on all sides with flour and brown chops in oil.

4. Add onions and mushrooms and sauté until tender. Cover.

5. Pour gravy over chops and blend in salt and pepper.

6. Simmer on low for 20 minutes or until chops are tender.

Smothered pork chops are an old-fashioned southern favorite. They are easy to prepare and are packed with tons of flavor.

# PAN-FRIED **MACKEREL CAKES**

1 15oz CAN MACKEREL, DEBONED

½ SMALL ONION, CHOPPED

1 EGG, BEATEN

½ CUP ITALIAN FLAVORED BREAD CRUMBS

¼ TEASPOON SALT

¼ TEASPOON GROUND BLACK PEPPER

½ TEASPOON WORCESTERSHIRE SAUCE

5 TABLESPOONS CANOLA OIL

*This was one of my favorites for breakfast growing up. My mother would serve it with eggs and toast. This is a great alternative to bacon and sausage.*

1. Mix mackerel, onion, salt, pepper, egg, and Worcestershire sauce in medium bowl.

2. Form 6 patties approximately 1 inch thick.

3. Preheat oil in pan.

4. Coat patties on all sides with bread crumbs.

5. Add patties to pan and slowly brown them on both sides.

[SERVES 3]

# SUNDAY BRUNCH **CRAB CAKES**

1 LB CRAB MEAT

2 STALKS SCALLIONS, CHOPPED

4 TABLESPOONS BUTTER, MELTED

2 EGGS, BEATEN

½ CUP CRUSHED CRACKERS

½ CUP BREAD CRUMBS

1 TEASPOON WORCESTERSHIRE SAUCE

½ TEASPOON SALT

¼ TEASPOON GROUND BLACK PEPPER

¼ TEASPOON CAYENNE PEPPER

2 TABLESPOONS CANOLA OIL

[SERVES 4]

1. Mix crab meat, scallions, butter, crackers, Worcestershire, salt, pepper, cayenne, and eggs together.

2. Preheat oil in pan over medium heat.

3. Form mixture into small cakes. Coat cakes on all sides with bread crumbs.

4. Place cakes in pan and brown on both sides, about 5 minutes.

For Sauce:

2/3 cup mayonnaise

splash Tabasco sauce

1 teaspoon Worcestershire sauce

4 tablespoons dijon mustard

1 tablespoon ketchup

1 teaspoon lemon juice

2 scallions, chopped

2 tablespoons parsley, chopped

1 tablespoon paprika

1/2 teaspoon kosher salt

1/8 teaspoon ground black pepper

Whisk all of the ingredients together in a small bowl and refrigerate until ready to serve.

# PAN-FRIED **SALMON**

**4 MEDIUM SALMON FILLETS**

**½ TEASPOON GROUND BLACK PEPPER**

**1 TEASPOON CREOLE SEASONING**

**1½ CUPS SEAFOOD BREADER**

**2 TABLESPOONS CANOLA OIL**

1. Preheat oil in frying pan over medium heat.

2. Season both sides of salmon with pepper and Creole seasoning.

3. Coat salmon with breader and place in frying pan.

4. Brown salmon on both sides, about 5 minutes each side.

5. Remove salmon and drain on paper towel covered plate.

[SERVES 4]

# SUCCULENT **ROAST CHICKEN**

1 6-7 LB OVEN ROASTER

2 TABLESPOONS BUTTER, MELTED

1 TEASPOON SALT

½ TEASPOON GROUND BLACK PEPPER

1 ENVELOPE VEGETABLE SOUP MIX

10 HOLLAND-STYLE ONIONS, HALVED

4oz MUSHROOMS, SLICED

1 CUP CHICKEN STOCK

[SERVES 4-6]

**1.** Preheat oven to 425°. Remove all contents from the chicken cavity. Rinse chicken inside and outside with cold water. Dry chicken with paper towels. Season the cavity of the chicken with salt and pepper.

**2.** Place chicken in the center of a roasting pan. Tuck wing tips under the body of the chicken.

**3.** Spread the butter over surface of chicken and top with onions and mushrooms. Sprinkle with vegetable soup mix. Pour stock into bottom of pan.

**4.** Place in oven, and roast until skin is golden brown and crispy or about 1 1/2 hours. Insert an instant-read thermometer into the breast. The temperature should read 180° and the juice that runs out should be clear.

**5.** Baste chicken with juice from bottom of pan. Carve and serve.

# LEMON-PEPPER **CHICKEN**

1 CHICKEN, SECTIONED

2/3 CUP LEMON JUICE, ROOM TEMP.

½ CUP BUTTER, MELTED, ROOM TEMP.

1 TEASPOON YELLOW MUSTARD

1 TEASPOON GRANULATED SUGAR

¼ TEASPOON GARLIC POWDER

½ TEASPOON SALT

¼ TEASPOON GROUND BLACK PEPPER

¼ CUP VIRGIN OLIVE OIL

[SERVES 4]

1. Rinse chicken and pat dry with paper towels.

2. Preheat oil in pan over medium heat.

3. Season chicken with salt and pepper.

4. Place chicken in pan and brown chicken on both sides.

5. Blend remaining ingredients in small bowl.

6. Pour lemon sauce over chicken, cover, and simmer for 30 minutes or until chicken is tender.

*My grandmother ate lemon pepper chicken a few times each week. This dish is quick and easy. It is ready in less than 1 hour!*

# SOULFUL SIDES

# BAKED **MACARONI & CHEESE**

**3 CUPS MACARONI NOODLES**

**2 CUPS MILK**

**½ CUP ALL PURPOSE FLOUR**

**1 EGG, BEATEN**

**½ STICK BUTTER, MELTED**

**3½ CUPS SHARP CHEDDAR, SHREDDED**

**2 CUPS COLBY JACK, SHREDDED**

**1 TEASPOON SEASONED SALT**

**½ TEASPOON GROUND BLACK PEPPER**

[10 SERVINGS]

1. Cook noodles until tender and then drain.

2. In large saucepan, melt butter over medium heat. Add milk, flour, and egg. Blend well.

3. Add salt, pepper, colby jack, and two cups of cheddar. Blend well.

4. Preheat oven to 350°. Combine noodles and cheese sauce in large pot.

5. Slightly grease casserole dish. Pour noodles into dish and top with remaining cheddar.

6. Bake for 30 mintues or until cheese becomes a crust.

# ANGELIC **EGGS**

12 HARD-BOILED EGGS, HALVED

½ CUP MAYONNAISE

½ TEASPOON SALT

¼ TEASPOON GROUND BLACK PEPPER

1 TABLESPOON GRANULATED SUGAR

1 TABLESPOON YELLOW MUSTARD

2 STALKS SCALLIONS, CHOPPED

1 STALK CELERY, FINELY CHOPPED

¼ CUP SWEET SALAD CUBES

1. Remove egg yolks.

2. Blend yolks, mayonnaise, salt, pepper, sugar, mustard, scallions, celery, and salad cubes in large bowl.

3. Evenly fill eggs with filling.

4. Chill before serving, then garnish with lightly sprinkled paprika.

[SERVES 12]

Deviled eggs were a staple in my household. growing up. on any holiday or at any gathering we had. My mom did a lot of entertaining. When she had her Tupperware parties, birthdays, showers or any other type of gathering, she would serve deviled eggs.. They are very simple to make and most people like them. I call them Angelic Eggs becasue something so good couldn't be of the devil.

# BLACK-EYED **PEAS**

16oz FROZEN BLACK-EYED PEAS

1 SMOKED TURKEY DRUMSTICK, DEBONED

1 MEDIUM ONION, CHOPPED

1 12oz CAN DICED ROASTED TOMATOES

1 MEDIUM GREEN PEPPER, DICED

1 TEASPOON SEASONED SALT

½ TEASPOON GROUND BLACK PEPPER

3 CUPS CHICKEN BROTH

[SERVES 8-10]

1. Add the peas, turkey, tomatoes, green pepper, salt, pepper and broth to a large pot.

2. Cover and cook over medium heat for 45 minutes to 1 hour, or until the peas are tender. Add additional broth, if necessary.

3. Serve garnished with crumbled bacon.

Black-eyed peas before being cooked!

# LOADED **MASHED POTATOES**

**6 LARGE POTATOES, DICED, SKIN ON**

**½ CUP MILK**

**½ CUP BUTTER, MELTED**

**¼ CUP CHIVES, CHOPPED**

**½ CUP BACON, CRUMBLED**

**1 CUP CHEDDAR CHEESE, SHREDDED**

**½ CUP SOUR CREAM**

**½ TEASPOON SALT**

**1 TEASPOON GROUND BLACK PEPPER**

[SERVES 8]

1. In 4-quart saucepan, cover potatoes with water and bring to a boil.

2. Simmer for 20 minutes or until potatoes are tender.

3. Drain and slightly mash.

4. Stir in remaining ingredients.

When people eat baked potatoes, they usually just eat the insides. What they don't realize is that many of the nutrients are in the skin. This is a great tasting way to incorporate the whole potato.

# SWEET & SPICY **BAKED BEANS**

1 3LB CAN PORK & BEANS

½ MEDIUM VIDALIA ONION, CHOPPED

½ GREEN PEPPER, CHOPPED

1 TABLESPOON YELLOW MUSTARD

3 STRIPS BACON, SLICED INTO 12 PIECES

½ CUP TOMATO SAUCE

½ TEASPOON WORCESTERSHIRE SAUCE

1/3 CUP DARK BROWN SUGAR

1/3 CUP MOLASSES

¾ TEASPOON CAYENNE PEPPER

2 TEASPOONS TABASCO SAUCE

[SERVES 8]

1. Preheat oven to 300°.

2. Mix all ingredients in medium bowl and pour into medium casserole dish.

3. Lay bacon on top and bake for 1 - 1½ hours.

# SOUTHERN-STYLE **COLLARD GREENS**

3 LBS COLLARD GREENS, SLICED

MEAT OF 2 SMOKED TURKEY DRUMSTICKS

¼ CUP SEASONED SALT

1½ TEASPOONS RED PEPPER

1 CUP GRANULATED SUGAR

3 CUPS CHICKEN BROTH

[SERVES 8]

1. Thoroughly rinse greens and drain in large colander.

2. Heat turkey and broth in large pot over medium-high heat. Bring to boil. Reduce heat to low and simmer until turkey is tender, about 30 minutes.

3. Add greens, salt, red pepper, and sugar. Stir together.

4. Cover pot and cook on low until tender, about 45 minutes, stirring occasionally.

5. Add more broth if it gets too low. Serve hot.

# SWEET POTATO CASSEROLE

3 CUPS SWEET POTATOES, PEELED, COOKED & SLICED

1 CUP GRANULATED SUGAR

1½ STICKS BUTTER, MELTED

1½ TEASPOONS VANILLA FLAVORING

3 EGGS, BEATEN

½ CUP MILK

½ CUP ALL PURPOSE FLOUR

¾ CUP LIGHT BROWN BROWN SUGAR

1 CUP PECANS, CHOPPED

[SERVES 8-10]

1. Blend potatoes, 2/3 of butter, sugar, vanilla, eggs, and milk in a large bowl.

2. Preheat oven to 375°.

3. Mix flour, brown sugar, pecans, and remaining butter in medium bowl.

4. In medium casserole dish, add potatoes and top with pecan mixture.

5. Bake for 45 minutes.

The best sweet potato casserole I have ever had was made by my Great-Uncle Eddie (Major Eddie L. Benns)! I will never cook it as well as him, but this is a close second!

The Process -->

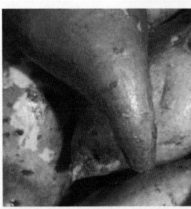

# ROASTED **ASPARAGUS**

**2 LBS FRESH ASPARAGUS**

**½ MEDIUM ONION, CHOPPED**

**VIRGIN OLIVE OIL**

**KOSHER SALT**

**GROUND BLACK PEPPER**

**[SERVES 8]**

*A few simple ingredients blended together provide the right flavor for asparagus. This dish makes an excellent side for most chicken, beef, and fish entrees.*

1. Preheat oven to 425°.

2. Cut off tough ends of the asparagus.

3. Place asparagus on baking sheet, drizzle with olive oil, then toss to coat completely.

4. Spread asparagus in single layer, top with onions, and sprinkle with salt and pepper to taste.

5. Roast the asparagus for 25 minutes, until tender but still crisp.

# JALAPEÑO CHEDDAR **CORN BREAD**

**1 PACKAGE CORN MUFFIN MIX**

**1 EGG, BEATEN**

**1/3 CUP MILK**

**1 STICK BUTTER, MELTED**

**1 TABLESPOON SUGAR**

**1 CUP SHARP CHEDDAR, SHREDDED**

**¼ CUP DICED JALAPEÑO PEPPERS**

**[SERVES 4-8]**

1. Preheat oven to 400°.

2. Line 8 muffin cups with a paper baking cup.

3. Combine all ingredients and blend well.

4. Pour into cups and bake for 20 minutes.

# SATISFYING SALADS

# GRACIOUS **CHICKEN SALAD**

ROTISSERIE CHICKEN, CHOPPED

2 CUPS RED & WHITE SEEDLESS GRAPES, HALVED

½ CUP PECANS, CHOPPED

2 STALKS SCALLIONS, CHOPPED

1 TABLESPOON MUSTARD

½ CUP MAYONNAISE

½ CUP SOUR CREAM

1 TEASPOON GROUND BLACK PEPPER

1 TEASPOON SALT

2 TABLESPOONS GRANULATED SUGAR

1. Stir together mustard, mayonnaise, sour cream, pepper, salt, and sugar in a large bowl.

2. Add chicken, grapes, and scallions, stir gently.

3. Cover and refrigerate for an hour.

4. Fold in pecans prior to serving.

[15 SERVINGS]

This was another traditional dish in my household growing up. My spin on this classic dish is to use a precooked rotisserie chicken. This adds a punch of flavor and saves you some preparation time.

# TANGY COLE SLAW

½ **HEAD GREEN CABBAGE, SHREDDED**

½ **HEAD RED CABBAGE, SHREDDED**

2 **CARROTS, PEELED & SHREDDED**

1 **SMALL VIDALIA ONION, CHOPPED**

½ **CUP MAYONNAISE**

¼ **CUP DIJON MUSTARD**

2 **TEASPOONS APPLE CIDER VINEGAR**

½ **CUP GRANULATED SUGAR**

1 **TEASPOON GROUND BLACK PEPPER**

½ **TEASPOON SALT**

[SERVES 8]

1. In large bowl, combine cabbage, carrots and onions.

2. In separate bowl, stir mayonnaise, mustard, vinegar, sugar, pepper, and salt together until well blended.

3. Toss dressing mixture with cabbage mixture.

4. Cover and refrigerate for 2-3 hours.

5. Serve cold.

# AUNT GRACE'S **7 LAYER SALAD**

**1 HEAD OF GREEN LEAF LETTUCE**

**PURPLE ONION, SLICED IN THIN RINGS**

**3-5 STALKS CELERY, SLICED BITE SIZED**

**12oz FROZEN UNCOOKED GREEN PEAS**

**MAYONNAISE**

**20 SLICES COOKED BACON, CRUMBLED**

**2 CUPS PARMESAN CHEESE**

**[SERVES 10]**

1. In large, deep, transparent dish, lay in layer of lettuce, onions, celery, peas, mayonnaise, bacon, and parmesan.

2. Refrigerate overnight or for 8 hours.

*Pat lettuce dry before tearing apart for salad.

*Freshly grated parmesan is preferred.

The first time I ever tried this amazing salad was during a family reunion in North Carolina. My Great-Aunt Grace made it and it was devoured within minutes. Everything tasted so fresh. The key to this freshness is preparing the salad according to the recipe and serving it immediately.

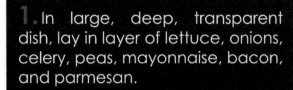

# GRANDMA'S **POTATO SALAD**

3 LBS RED RUSSET POTATOES, DICED

3 STALKS CELERY, FINELY CHOPPED

6 HARD-BOILED EGGS, CHOPPED

3 STALKS SCALLIONS, CHOPPED

½ CUP SWEET PICKLE CUBES

½ CUP YELLOW MUSTARD

1 CUP MAYONNAISE

1 TEASPOON GRANULATED SUGAR

2 TABLESPOONS SALT

2 TEASPOONS GROUND BLACK PEPPER

PAPRIKA

[SERVES 12-15]

1. Mix ingredients in large bowl.

2. Chill before serving.

# JUMBO SHRIMP **PASTA SALAD**

3 CUPS BOW-TIE PASTA, COOKED

1½ LBS COOKED, PEELED,
& DEVEINED JUMBO SHRIMP

½ CUP CELERY, DICED

½ CUP RED ONION, DICED

½ CUP GREEN PEPPER, DICED

½ CUP BLACK OLIVES, SLICED

10 CHERRY TOMATOES, QUARTERED

½ CUP LEMON JUICE

½ CUP VIRGIN OLIVE OIL

2 TABLESPOONS HONEY

1 TEASPOON DRIED THYME

¼ TEASPOON KOSHER SALT

¼ TEASPOON GROUND BLACK PEPPER

[SERVES 8-10]

1. In a large bowl combine all ingredients and blend well.

2. Cover with plastic wrap and chill for 2 hours.

3. Stir before serving.

# DELICIOUS DESSERTS

# NITA'S **BANANA PUDDING**

1 CUP GRANULATED SUGAR

2/3 CUP ALL PURPOSE FLOUR

¼ TEASPOON SALT

6 EGG YOLKS, BEATEN

4 CUPS MILK

1 TEASPOON VANILLA

1 BOX NILLA WAFERS

10 RIPE BANANAS, SLICED

1 LB WHIPPED CREAM

**1.** Mix sugar, flour, and salt in top of double boiler. Blend in egg yolks and milk.

**2.** Cook, uncovered, over boiling water 20 to 25 minutes or until thickened, stirring constantly.

**3.** Remove from heat; stir in vanilla.

**4.** Spread small amount of custard onto bottom of container; cover with layer of wafers and sliced bananas. Pour more custard over bananas. If using a large container, continue to layer wafers, bananas and custard to make a total of 3 layers of each, ending with custard.

**5.** Top with whipped cream, cool, and garnish with crushed wafers just before serving.

[SERVES 10-12]

When I was five, my grandmother began having me help her make banana pudding. I helped her by bringing her the ingredients. I also kneeled in a chair to measure the ingredients for her since I couldn't reach the table. She taught me that the key is to make your own custard instead of using boxed pudding. She said that little things like this show people that you love them. After she passed away, I didn't have anyone to make banana pudding with. I finally decided to make it myself. When my grandfather tasted it, he said it tasted just like my grandmother's!

# LOVER'S **COBBLER**

1 LB FRUIT (PEACHES, APPLES, BLUEBER-
RIES, OR CHERRIES)

2 STICKS UNSALTED BUTTER

¼ CUP NUTS, SLICED (ALMONDS,
WALNUTS, OR PECANS)

1 BOX BUTTER YELLOW CAKE MIX

1 TABLESPOON GROUND CINNAMON

½ TEASPOON GROUND NUTMEG

2 TABLESPOONS GRANULATED SUGAR

[SERVES 10]

*Have you ever heard the phrase "The way to a man's heart is through his stomach?" I don't know if it's true, nor do I care. What I do know is if you want to impress your honey before Valentine's Day or your birthday, prepare this simple dish. You will literally have them eating from the palm of your hand.*

1. Preheat oven to 375°.

2. In a 9x13 pan, layer fruit evenly and sprinkle nuts on top.

3. Evenly cover with cinnamon, nutmeg, and sugar.

4. Cover mixture completely with cake mix. (Crush lumps with fork.)

5. Slice butter and lay slices equal distance apart on top of cake mix.

6. Bake for 50 minutes. (Mixture should brown and firm.)

7. Serve hot and garnish with vanilla ice cream for unbelievable results.

# SWEET POTATO PIE

2 CUPS SWEET POTATOES, PEELED, COOKED & MASHED

1 STICK UNSALTED BUTTER, MELTED

2 EGGS, BEATEN

1 CUP MILK

¼ TEASPOON SALT

1 TEASPOON NUTMEG

½ CUP GRANULATED SUGAR

1 TEASPOON CINNAMON

1½ TEASPOONS VANILLA FLAVORING

1 9" PIE SHELL

[8 SERVINGS]

1. Preheat oven to 350°.

2. Cream potatoes with butter.

3. Beat eggs with sugar. Add potatoes, milk, salt, sugar, nutmeg, and cinnamon.

4. Pour filling in pie shell.

5. Bake for 45-50 minutes or until custard is set.

6. Top with whipped cream if preferred.

My Grandmother Juanita and Great-Aunt India, who was my grandfather's sister, made the best sweet potato pies I have ever tasted. I have never had a sweet potato pie as good as theirs. Aunt India made dozens of them at a time and froze them. When people stopped by, she would go to her freezer and give one to them to take home.

# INDEX

BLESSED & HIGHLY FLAVORED

Made in the USA
Charleston, SC
13 February 2013